MYSTIC
by the
A, B, "Sea"

Written and Illustrated by

Marion Kyff Dodd

FLAT HAMMOCK PRESS

FLAT
HAMMOCK
PRESS

A big thanks to my mother-in-law Beverly Dodd
and my mother Elizabeth Wise
for their valued suggestions and editing.

Text and Illustrations Copyright © 2006 Marion Kyff Dodd

The Publisher, Flat Hammock Press, 5 Church Street, Mystic, CT 06355

ISBN978-0-9773725-2-2

10 9 8 7 6 5 4 3 2

PRINTED IN THE UNITED STATES OF AMERICA

For my grandmother
whose cottage on the Connecticut shore
filled my childhood with wonderful memories
and inspired my love for the ocean.
-MKD

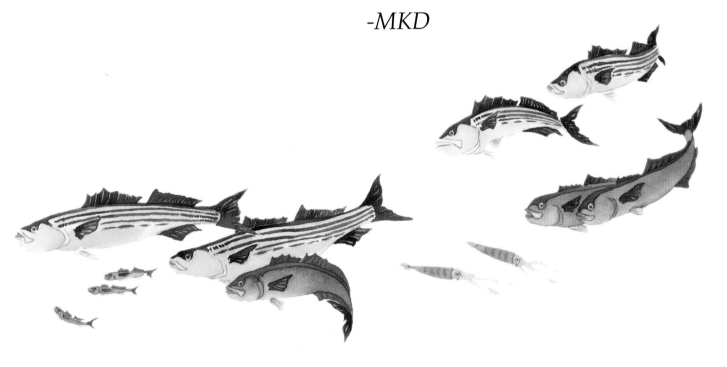

The little town of Mystic was built on Connecticut's shore.
I visit my grandparents' cottage there; It's summer fun galore!
Here's a book to show you all the wonderful things to see:
The ocean, the shore, the ships of old, it's a Mystic A,B,C.

A is for **aquarium**, home to creatures of the sea.
Harbor seals and beluga whales frolic and splash with glee.
Inside you'll find sharks, fish and rays in places where they dwell.
They even save poor injured seals and release them when they're well.

B is for the **bascule bridge** that rises up and down.
It crosses Mystic River which flows north and south through town.
"Bascule" in French means "seasaw" and that word describes it well.
Huge weights pull down, the bridge goes up; we hear the warning bell!

C is for the **Crabbing** we do hanging from the dock.
Snappy green crabs hide below thick seaweed and hard rock.
We lure them out with smelly bait tied to rocks with string.
Be patient and watch carefully. Quick! Scooping nets must swing!

D is for bold **draggers** in the commercial fishing fleet.
Traveling to rich fishing grounds is a most courageous feat.
Giant waves come crashing down, ice coats the rails and deck.
But fish must quickly get to market, the nets must all be checked.

E is for **explorers** diving deep to take a peek.
Seeking treasure from ancient times and creatures quite unique.
Robots gather prizes and take pictures of the ocean floor.
We visit the Aquarium to see what they've found and more.

F is for the agile **fish** that fill the waters here:
Blues and stripers at rocky reefs,
shad near shady piers.
Poppers or bait, swimmers or eels:
All fishermen have their tricks,
Cast out the line, gently feel the tug, set the hook,
Quick! Quick!

G is for the **galleries**, all filled with colorful art,
We see lovely paintings and sculptures each created from the heart.
I look to find the special stories that each piece portrays
Of summer flowers, sparkling seas
and sailboats on the bays.

H is for the **hay wagon** we ride at the country farm.
The quaint farmhouse and old rock walls have such a magical charm.
We ride through fields of swaying corn, ripening on their stalks.
Cows and sheep eat grass for lunch while the silly chickens squawk.

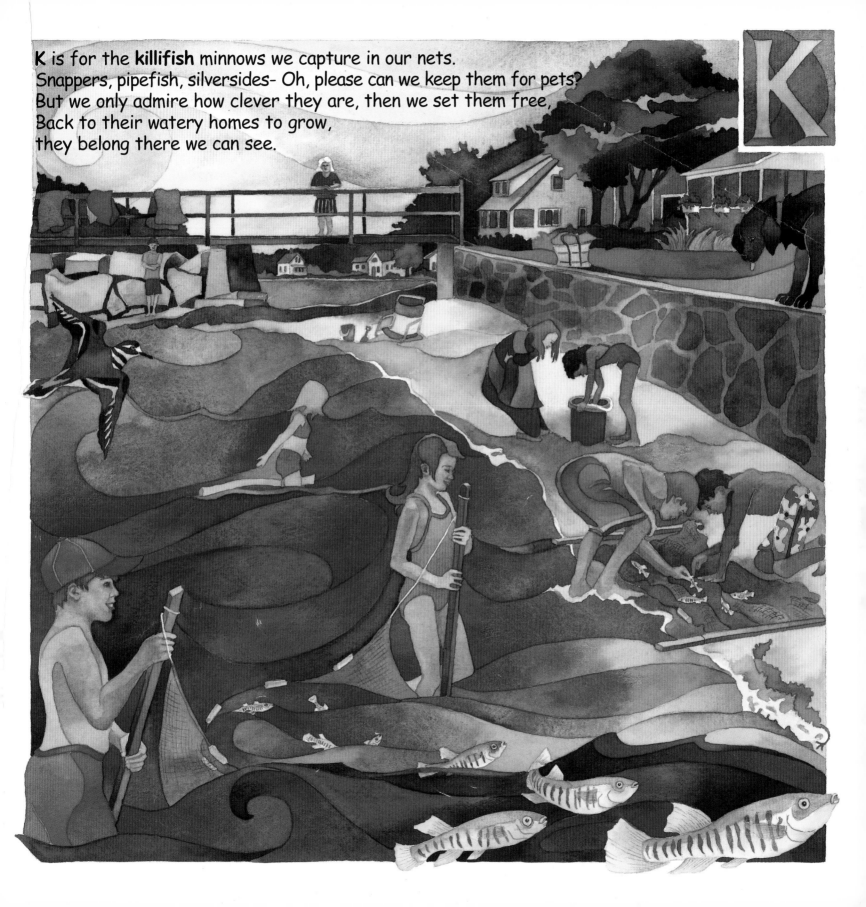

K is for the **killifish** minnows we capture in our nets.
Snappers, pipefish, silversides- Oh, please can we keep them for pets?
But we only admire how clever they are, then we set them free,
Back to their watery homes to grow,
they belong there we can see.

L is for **luscious lobsters** and **lobstermen** with their traps.
They pull up these spry treasures
sporting claws and a tail that flaps.
Their boats bring in the feisty catch for many a lobsterfest.
Some say clam chowder's their favorite, but I like lobster best.

M is for **moonjellies**, glowing softly in pale moonlight.
Bobbing blissfully in the waves, drifting through the night.
These creatures make pale nightlights and the sight can be quite grand.
As waves wash them ashore, they look like bubbles on the sand.

N is for the **Nature Center** with a pond and bubbling brook.
We quickly scoop nets in the pond then take a careful look.
Crayfish, tadpoles, turtles, snakes, spiders and dragonflies,
Hike through woods and buzzing fields: there's always some surprise!

O is for the **Old Lighthouse Museum** still standing proud and tall.
In 1814, the British tried to make this old town fall.
In this lighthouse are cannonballs British ships shot into town.
They wanted to gain old Stonington for the mighty English crown.
Defenders with only cannons three, made the ships retreat.
No lives were lost, no houses burned; They chased away that fleet!

P is for the **planetarium** which shows the sky at night.
Planets, stars and galaxies are made with a special light.
It is really dark inside as, many bright stars move by,
Venus, Big Dipper and Leo, all glowing in the sky.

S is for the **Seaport**, a small village from an earlier time.
It's set in the 1800's; whaling was at its prime.
Craftsmen here built sturdy ships that sailed the seven seas.
We learn how people lived without cars or electricity.

T is for the **towering tall ships** lining the Seaport's docks.
Explore cramped rooms where seamen lived as the old boat gently rocks.
Large masts reach skyward covered with sails flapping in the wind.
Sailors climb to lofty heights if a torn one needs a mend.

U is for the bright **umbrellas** placed up and down our beach.
Children dashing in the waves. They run and splash and screech.
Sandcastles are built carefully adorned with marine décor.
Chatter fills the salty air, as noisy seagulls soar.

U

V is for the **village** where quaint shops line a small path.
A pond lies in the middle; Ducks use it as a bath.
We feed the ducks and ducklings as the waterwheel goes round.
The shoppers rest on benches and show keepsakes that they've found.

W is for the **wily whalers** who sailed through storms and plight.
Hunting whales for precious oil that lit up Mystic's nights.
Many years might go by before their voyage brought them home.
They often passed time singing or whittling old whale bones.

X is for "X-marks-the-spot" where hidden treasure lies.
Pillage, plunder, steal and loot; these pirates weren't nice guys.
Captain Kidd would visit Mystic to think, relax and play.
Treasure of his was found nearby, more is buried here they say.

Y is for the old time **yachts** drifting on the gentle tide.
Moving slowly down the river in a carefree, festive glide.
Flags are flying, colors showing, there's music in the air.
We see an antique boat parade, a rollicking fanfare.

Z is for the **zigzags**: sailboats tacking back and forth.
Cutting through the salty waves going up the river- north!
Sailing school boats fill the river and laughter fills the air,
Sea mist sprays upon our faces as wind whips through our hair.

My summer visit's over but I'm sure you will agree,
Why this village is called Mystic; It's magic by the sea!
Excitement on each corner; There is history everywhere.
Soft ocean breezes beckon; many memories we can share.